Fashion Desi Sketchbook

Women's Wear Fashion Illustration templates. 9 heads tall figure.

by Irina V. Ivanova

- eight fashion figures of the same style
- single (one per page) figures as well as group arrangements (in groups of two and three figures)
- light grey color for easy sketching over the figures
- three-quarter view, back view, and side view included
- mild movement and static still poses

Art Design Project, Inc

Fashion Design Sketchbook
Women's Wear Fashion Illustration templates. 9 heads tall figure.

For permission for additional use please contact Permissions, Art Design Project, Inc. www.artdesignproject.com/permissions.html

ISBN: 9781731229861
Book Website
www.fashioncroquis .com
Email: contact@atdesignproject.com

Give feedback on the book at:
contact@atdesignproject.com

Art Design Project, Incorporated

Printed in U.S.A

About the author

Irina V. Ivanova is a Florida-based educator, fashion illustrator, and visual artist. Irina delights in merging her versatile professional life experiences in a blend of fashion, art, and teaching.

As a fashion illustrator, Irina combines her profound knowledge of clothing design with artistry. In her books, Irina balancing creative and technical aspects of fashion process.

Art and fashion in Irina V. Ivanova's book Art and fashion merged in Irina's books helping each other for the benefit of a reader.

Irina's books are not just "beautiful" books about fashion. Irina's books are practical guides on fashion subjects and collection of practical resources articulated with artistic talent and illustration skill. Her fashion drawing books are real-world practical and, in the meantime, artistically stylish way.

contact Irina V. Ivanova via the website
www.ivanova.studio
www.ivanova.studio/contactus.shtml

Haute Couture Fashion Illustration Resource Book

Subtitle: _How to draw evening dresses and wedding gowns_

ISBN-13: 978-0984356034
ISBN-10: 0984356037
Page count: 261 pages
Trim Size:11" x 8.5" (21.59cm x 27.94cm)
Color: Black and White
Paper/material: White paper
Publisher: Art Design Project, Inc.
Publication date: 2018-09-16
Author: Irina V. Ivanova

This is a book for everyone who designs, illustrates or works with "haute couture style" fashion. If you need to illustrate wedding dresses, evening gowns, one of a kind outfits loosely covered by a term "haute couture", this book is for you. With the Haute Couture Fashion Illustration Resource Book, you will

Be more productive. This is a book for busy professionals who value their time and effort. The book includes figure drawing templates, so you do not have to draw your fashion illustration from scratch! Select a croquis from the book and sketch over it.

Jump start your project! This book breaks through creative blocks by offering ideas of dress silhouettes and inspiring step by step drawing demos.

Be focused on the practical aspects of fashion design. You need to illustrate your dress with an understanding of sewing and fabrics. All illustrations of the dress elements in this book were created with the expert knowledge of Haute Couture construction.

Learn how to draw accurately. All drawings in this book are simple pencil drawings, with step by step demos which makes it easier to see the illustration process.

Learn visually. Are you a visual learner? Then this book is for you! The book has almost no text, just terms, and captions. This is not a book to read; it is a tool to practice.

Stay focused on details. In many cases, haute couture style dress is all about intricate details. To draw complex design elements accurately and fast could be an intimidating task. This book contains a series of clearly depicted details. With this book on your desk, it is easier to get your project done.

Children's wear fashion illustration resource book

Subtitle: *Children's figure drawing templates with fashion design sketches*

ISBN-13:978-0692554074
ISBN-10:0692554076
Page count:132 pages
Trim Size: 8.5" x 11" (21.59cm x 27.94cm)
Color: Black and White
Paper/material: White paper
Publisher: Art Design Project, Inc.
Publication date: 2015-11-12
Language: English

Author: Irina V. Ivanova

- Children's Wear Fashion Illustration Resource Book is a practical aid for fashion drawing. There are 40 figure drawing templates for 4 different age groups, complemented with multiple sketches and illustrations. All figures are shown in front, back, three-quarter and side views.

- The book is very visual - you can see the main steps of the drawing process for each illustration.

- There is no text in the book other than captions, a short introduction and a brief summary. The book is designed to be a visual aid for fashion illustration of children's wear. Figure templates, raw sketches and accomplished fashion illustration is the main content of the book.

- The book is very instructive and practical. Sketches are created from the templates and turned into finished illustrations. All drawings are made with simple pencil only. Roughness and sketchiness of these drawings is carefully preserved. Trace a template from the book and draw fashion sketches with the template. Fashion sketching with the book is less stressful and tends to smooth the designer's work flow.

- The book shows how to sketch on a figure and how to turn a sketch into a completed illustration.

- Choose a figure for your project from the selection of age groups and body movements. There are sets of ready to use figures for 0- 1, 1-3, 4-6 and 7-10 years old children. The templates in the book designed to show apparel from any sides with various poses and movements.

- Book combines visuals of garment details with basic terminology as written captions. Such "visual dictionary" component enhances the book's usefulness as a designer's reference resource.

How to draw fashion flats

Subtitle: A practical guide to fashion technical *drawing (pencil and marker techniques)*

ISBN-13: 978-0984356027
ISBN-10: 0984356029
Page count: 214 pages
Trim Size:11" x 8.5" (21.59cm x 27.94cm)
Color: Black and White
Paper/material: White paper
Publisher: Art Design Project, Inc.
Publication date: 2016-09-30
Language: English
Author: Irina V. Ivanova

- Draw fashion flats with easiness. Book saves time and makes the complexity of technical drawing easy to comprehend.

Who should use this book?

- Independent designer or small business professional. Be more efficient by making the process of creating and correcting flats easier and more reliable.
- Professionals in the field of fashion design, apparel technical design and garment product development.
- Fashion merchandising professionals. Use the book as a reference for garment elements terms and a glossary of garment types.
- Students who study fashion design, patternmaking and fashion merchandising.

What is in the book?

- Step-by-step guides on how to draw pants, t-shirts, jackets, swimwear, and skirts.
- Do's and don'ts, the right and wrong examples (visuals with captions).
- Visual galleries of garment details.
- Main fashion apparel terms illustrated.
- Drawing tips from the expert.
- Figure templates for drawing flats.

Use the figure templates to draw your flats. Women, men, children (4 different age groups) as well as a plus size women and big and tall man figures.
- The gallery of completed projects. Learn the main steps of development flats from sketches. The gallery shows fashion illustrations with matching flats and work sketches.

The book focuses on pencil and marker techniques with rulers and French curves. This expert, hands-on guide makes essential basic concepts of fashion flats easy to understand. Text in the book is concise and to-the-point. More than 700 hand drawn visuals are in the book to illustrate every step, every term, and every concept. It is a unique book, created by a professional for professionals.

Men's wear fashion illustration resource book

Subtitle: Figure drawing templates with fashion design sketches (pencil drawing techniques)

ISBN-13:978-0692608647
ISBN-10:0692608648
Page count: 184 pages
Trim Size: 8.5" x 11" (21.59cm x 27.94cm)
Color: Black and White
Paper/material: White paper
Publisher: Art Design Project, Inc.
Publication date: 2017-05-29
Language: English
Author: Irina V. Ivanova

Who should use this book?

- Independent men's wear designers or small business professional working for the menswear market.
- Professionals in the field of fashion design, apparel technical design and garment product development for menswear.
- Fashion merchandising professionals interested in menswear.
- Students who study fashion design, patternmaking and fashion merchandising.

What is in the book?

- Templates: men's figures, faces and hair styles.
- Step by step process of drawing menswear on the croquis.
- How to draw men's t-shirt, dress shirt, casual jacket, boxy jacket, sweaters, shorts, hats.
- Mix and match bottoms and tops for men's wear projects.
- Step by step fashion illustration process.
- Gallery of men's wear fashion drawing projects.
- Resources for drawing men's fashion accessories. Hats, neckwear, and shoes. Visuals and terms.
- Gallery of garment details relevant to men's wear. Visuals and terms.
- Gallery of sketches. A collection of sketched men's wear ideas.

What makes this book unique?

Figure drawing templates of the male figure. All templates are styled and designed for fashion illustration. There is no other book on the market with that many different poses for men's fashion figure.

Men's fashion illustration is a neglected subject and this book is trying to change it.

Preview from new upcoming book from the Fashion Croquis series by
Irina V. Ivanova:

women's wear. Sign up for updates at

www.fashioncroquis.com/signup.shtml

Feedback

If you are happy with your book, please take a minute to review it on
Amazon or send feedback directly to our team at
books@artdesignproject.com
or via web link www.fashioncroquis.com/contactus.html
Any feedback will be greatly appreciated.
Our team would be thrilled to hear back from you.
Thank you!!!!

Made in the USA
Coppell, TX
11 January 2024

27560343R00063